In Sweden

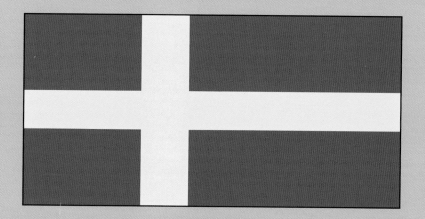

written by **Judy Zocchi** illustrated by **Neale Brodie**

dingles&company New Jersey

For Rocky & Robbin

First printing

PUBLISHED BY dingles&company
P.O. Box 508 • Sea Girt, New Jersey • 08750
WEBSITE: www.dingles.com • E-MAIL: info@dingles.com

Library of Congress Catalog Card No.: 2004096610
ISBN: 1-59646-087-3

Printed in the United States of America

ART DIRECTION & DESIGN BY Barbie Lambert
EDITED BY Andrea Curley
RESEARCH AND ADDITIONAL COPY WRITTEN BY Robert Neal Kanner
EDUCATIONAL CONSULTANT Bridget Riley Turnbach
PRE-PRESS BY Pixel Graphics

The Global Adventures series takes children on an around-the-world exploration of a variety of fascinating countries. The series examines each country's history and physical features as well as its most popular customs, activities, and foods.

Global Adventures

Judy Zocchi

is the author of the Global Adventures, Holiday Happenings, Click & Squeak's Computer Basics, and Paulie and Sasha series. She is a writer and lyricist who holds a bachelor's degree in fine arts/theater from Mount Saint Mary's College and a master's degree in educational theater from New York University. She lives in Manasquan, New Jersey, with her husband, David.

Neale Brodie

is a freelance illustrator who lives in Brighton, England, with his wife and young daughter. He is a self-taught artist, having received no formal education in illustration. As well as illustrating a number of children's books, he has worked as an animator in the computer games industry.

In Sweden people spend the KRONA.

Krona is the official currency of Sweden. One krona equals 100 ore. In English krona means crown.

CRYSTAL is made and sold worldwide.

Sweden was one of the first countries to make crystal and glass. The southeastern region of Sweden has approximately twenty world famous glassworks and is called the Kingdom of Crystal.

SWEDISH is
what people speak.

Swedish is the official language of Sweden.

What happened?
I went too fast on the turn.

An ICE HOTEL guest sleeps on a reindeer's hide.

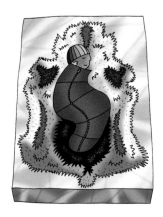

Every year since 1989 a hotel is built entirely of ice in Jukkasjarvi, a village in northern Sweden. It has an ice wedding chapel, an ice art exhibition hall, a movie theater with an ice screen, and rooms for more than 100 guests. The hotel only lasts for 6 months, though, because in summer it melts!

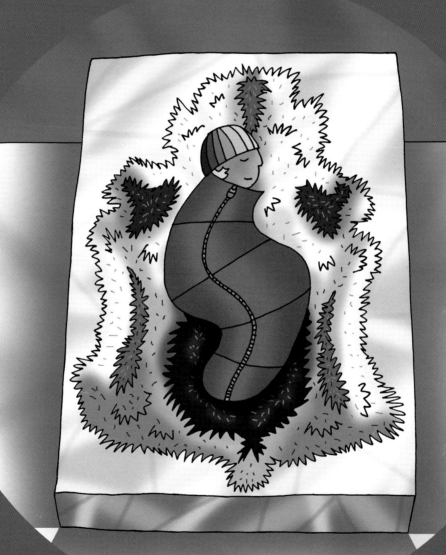

In Sweden
SAINT LUCIA'S DAY
is a favorite holiday.

Saint Lucia's Day is celebrated on December 13. Because she died at the time of year when nights begin to get shorter, Saint Lucia became a symbol of light to the Swedish people. The holiday also celebrates the coming of Christmas.

A SUMMERLAND is a popular outdoor gathering place.

This recreational area offers the entire family many activities, including swimming, row boating, bicycling, and water rides in beautifully landscaped surroundings.

The WOLVERINE is a cross between a weasel and a bear.

A member of the weasel family, wolverines walk on the soles of their feet just as bears do. When there is snow on the ground, their large, furry feet act like snowshoes, allowing the animal to move quickly to capture its prey.

A SMORGASBORD takes up lots of space.

This is a Swedish style of serving meals to large numbers of people, such as at a party. It usually consists of a long table set with a variety of dishes, such as herring (a type of small fish), meatballs, salmon, breads, salads, potatoes, and desserts.

In Sweden
DALA HORSES are brightly painted.

These carved wooden toy horses were first created by Swedish woodcutters in a region called Dalarna many centuries ago. The horses vary in size, with no two ever identical. They have become a traditional hand-crafted Swedish keepsake.

VASA is
an ancient ship.

In 1628 the Swedish king launched a large warship that was badly designed and sunk a short distance from shore. In 1961 the ship was brought up from the bottom of the ocean almost intact. It is on display in a museum in a Stockholm harbor.

Students wear WHITE HATS when they graduate.

In Sweden, a white cap is a traditional symbol of learning. Students who finish the Swedish equivalent of high school sometimes wear this traditional graduation cap during the graduation ceremony.

BLUEBERRY SOUP
is given
to skiers to sip.

This popular soup is made with fresh blueberries, water, sugar, and lemon. It is usually kept warm in a thermos and served on the slopes for refreshment.

Swedish culture is fun to learn.

KRONA
(KRO-na)

CRYSTAL

SWEDISH

ICE HOTEL

SAINT LUCIA'S DAY

SUMMERLAND

WOLVERINE

SMORGASBORD
(smor-gose-BORD)

DALA HORSES
(DAW-la)

VASA

WHITE HATS

BLUEBERRY SOUP

Jukkasjarvi: In this village 120 miles above the Arctic Circle you can stay in the world's biggest ice igloo hotel and sleep on beds built of ice, wood, and reindeer skin.

Stockholm: Here you can tour Kungliga Slottet, the largest residential royal castle in the world. It has more than 600 rooms.

Ystad: For 700 years, a watchman atop a church has blown his horn every quarter hour to tell residents of this medieval town that all is calm.

N W E S

NORWAY

SWEDEN

Jukkasjärvi

GULF OF BOTHNIA

FINLAND

Stockholm

Ystad

NORTH SEA

BALTIC SEA

See what you can discover at every turn!

OFFICIAL NAME:
Kingdom of Sweden

CAPITAL CITY:
Stockholm

CURRENCY:
Swedish krona

MAJOR LANGUAGE:
Swedish

BORDERS:
Finland, Gulf of Bothnia, Baltic Sea, Norway

CONTINENT:
Europe

ABOUT SWEDEN

The first inhabitants were hunter tribes who came from what is now Europe by way of a land bridge. In the 11th century, Norse people, or Vikings, who lived in the area controlled the river trade. They also went on expeditions to trade with or conquer other lands. In the 14th century, Sweden united with Norway and Denmark under one king but broke away in the 16th century. In 1809 Sweden became a constitutional monarchy (where the king's or queen's powers are limited by a set of rules, or constitution). Sweden remained neutral in both World War I and II. The country has about 90,000 lakes and is three-fifths forests. Fifteen percent of Sweden is north of the Arctic Circle. Major industries include lumbering, mining, and tourism. Sweden is known for its social welfare system, where the government provides social services for all of its citizens.

UNDERSTANDING AND CELEBRATING CULTURAL DIFFERENCES
• What do you have in common with children from Sweden?
• What things do you do differently from the children in Sweden?
• What is your favorite new thing you learned about Sweden?
• What unique thing about your culture would you like to share?

TRAVELING THROUGH SWEDEN
• Can you name the country that borders Sweden to the east?
• In which direction would you be traveling if you journeyed from Stockholm to Jonkoping?
• In which region of Sweden is the Arctic Circle located?

TRY SOMETHING NEW...
Have a Viking party and make your own hats. You can make a Viking hat from construction paper or a paper oatmeal canister. Don't forget to add horns! Then dress up in the type of clothing that Vikings might have worn.